Smithsonian

ELEPHANTS ON THE MOVE

A DAY WITH AN ASIAN ELEPHANT FAMILY

BY LELA NARGI

CAPSTONE EDITIONS
a capstone imprint

Pale morning sunlight spreads through the city of Washington, D.C. At the Smithsonian's National Zoo and Conservation Biology Institute, the animals stir in their habitats.
Birds chirp. Orangutans stretch.
Snakes slither.

The Asian elephants rumble, excited for the day. The animal keepers greet them by name.

GOOD MORNING, BOZIE!

GOOD MORNING, SWARNA AND SPIKE!

HELLO, KAMALA AND MAHARANI!

The elephants flap their ears to return the greeting.

MAHARANI, nicknamed **RANI**, is the youngest of the herd. She is smart and enjoys activities that make her think. Rani especially likes learning new behaviors that help keepers take care of her. If she doesn't understand a behavior they are asking for, she can get frustrated. She is a high achiever and is motivated by food—she eagerly accepts treats and praise from her keepers.

KAMALA is friendly, smart, and protective. She is Rani's mother, and she still watches over her "baby," even though Rani is full grown! Kamala is a quick learner and enjoys interacting with keepers. Sometimes, she sniffs their shoes, then rumbles and squeaks to let them know she's excited to see (and smell) them!

SWARNA is energetic and a bit anxious, but she aims to please her keepers. They help boost her confidence at times by asking her to do easier behaviors that she knows well. She enjoys playing with big sticks and will often chew on them or carry them around.

BOZIE is smart, social, busy, and feisty. She is slow to warm up to new keepers, but once they have earned her trust, she enjoys training with them. She often makes excited sounds like squeaking, honking, and trumpeting. Bozie is motivated by relationships. She will keep trying to get the attention she craves from both her keepers and elephant family.

SPIKE is usually laid back and easygoing. As the only male, or bull, of the herd, he is also the biggest at 9 feet (2.7 meters) tall and 13,000 pounds (5,900 kilograms)! In the wild, males spend a lot of time alone. But at the Zoo, Spike is quite social. He can often be found beside his pal Swarna.

A herd of Asian elephants bathes in a lake, cooling off on a hot day in Sri Lanka.

Rani and Spike were born in human care. Kamala, Bozie, and Swarna were rescued from the wild in Sri Lanka when, as youngsters, they were found separated from their families. An orphanage cared for them before they were sent to new homes.

Asian elephants come from Sri Lanka, India, Myanmar, Thailand, and other countries in Asia. Scientists who study Asian elephants say fewer than 50,000 are left in the wild.

The elephants living at the Smithsonian's National Zoo are helping their wild relatives. How can that be?

Each day, Zoo scientists learn more about Asian elephants from this little herd. They look at how elephants socialize, how they move and explore, and when and where they eat and sleep. They look for clues that the elephants are ready to mate. The scientists share what they learn with people in Asia who help protect wild elephants from threats like poaching, habitat loss, and conflicts with humans. Zoo visitors are also inspired to help protect wild elephants by getting to know the Zoo herd.

Scientists and keepers develop close bonds with the elephants in their care. They learn each elephant's personality, likes and dislikes, and particular needs.

Every day at the Zoo begins with breakfast. As the elephants gather, their keepers watch them closely. They look for any signs that the animals may be hurt or unwell. Keepers may call in the veterinary team to treat an elephant who's not behaving as usual.

The elephants lumber into the barn where a meal of hay and grain is waiting. Bozie lifts a trunkful of hay and tucks it into her mouth. Swarna shoves Spike to steal his hay. Spike doesn't mind. He's used to Swarna's playful tricks!

Rani would rather eat apples. Kamala stands nearby in case she has to soothe her. If things do not go Rani's way, she shows her feelings with big body movements and by banging on things around her.

Bozie and Rani snack on trunkfuls of hay.
Asian elephants are herbivores, or plant eaters.

MUNCH
MUNCH

A typical daily diet for an adult female elephant could total about 135 pounds (61 kg), consisting of about two-and-a-half bales of hay, 8 pounds (3.6 kg) of elephant chow, 2 pounds (0.9 kg) each of bran and oats, and 10 pounds (4.5 kg) of fruits and vegetables.

Next the keepers give the elephants their checkups. They look at their teeth to make sure they are clean and strong. They look in ears to make sure they are healthy. They also look at the elephants' skin, eyes, feet, and trunks. Keepers cannot see these things from far away. They teach the elephants to present their body parts so they can get an up-close look.

Keepers give the elephants pedicures and file their toenails. They also pry out anything that might have gotten stuck in the elephants' footpads.

Above, Swarna is trained to have dental X-rays. Examining teeth is a routine part of the keepers' daily health checks. They look for any redness, swelling, sharp edges, and changes in the wear pattern.

At right, a keeper checks an elephant's foot. Keepers inspect pads, cuticles, and nails, and trim them to prevent cracks. Foot care is important to elephant health.

The elephants seem to enjoy the attention during their health checks. But if an elephant doesn't feel like having its checkup in the morning, that's okay. The keepers will do it later, when the elephant is interested in taking part.

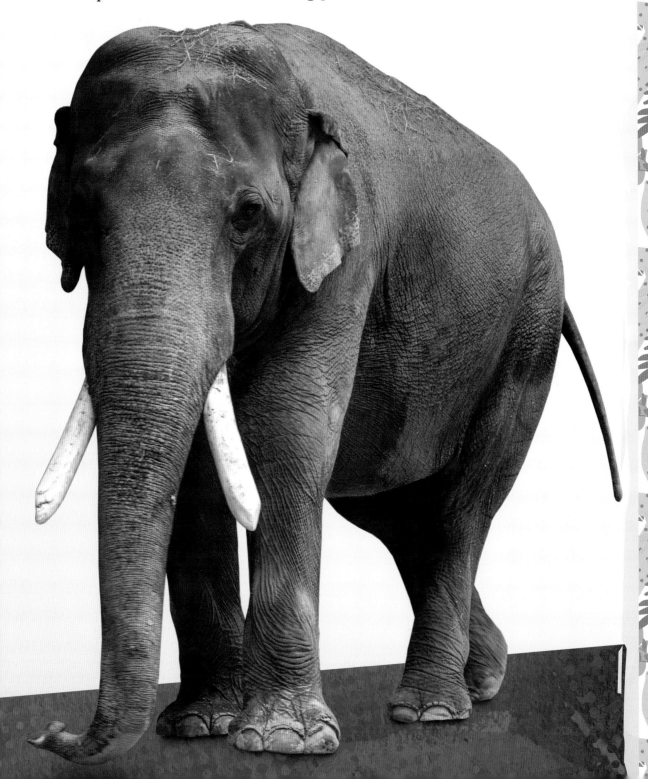

Then it's bath time. Keepers use scrub brushes with long handles to reach under and over the elephants to wash them. Once the dirt is scrubbed away, keepers can make sure the elephants' skin is clear and healthy. And the elephants get some nice back scratches!

There are several pools in the elephants' habitat. Throughout the day, the elephants might splash, lie down, and blow bubbles in the water to stay cool or just to have fun.

SPLASH!

After their baths, the Zoo herd takes a trek on the exercise trail. The ground on the trail is sloped, like it would be in a wild forest. This gives elephant legs good exercise.

Rani and Bozie stroll up and down the trail. They toss leaves and twigs and bellow loudly to each other.

Kamala walks slowly behind, followed by wide-eyed Swarna. They browse bamboo hanging along the trail, enjoying the shade and the breeze.

Spike keeps to himself until Swarna runs back to tease him.

A keeper offers a snack to Rani during her walk on the trek.

Along the way, the elephants might find small stashes of food that the keepers have hidden for them. Just like elephants that forage in the wild, the Zoo's elephants are challenged to find food in new places. These scavenger hunts encourage the elephants to explore. They are a form of enrichment.

SURPRISE SNACK

Keepers position feeders at different locations around the habitat. The feeders drop hay at various times throughout the day.

Enrichment is a way to keep elephant minds sharp. These clever creatures are curious about toys and tools they find to play with in their habitat. Elephants love discovering new things. But interacting with other elephants is the favorite type of enrichment of these social animals.

FRIENDLY HELLO!

Rani and Kamala shove a tractor tire dangling from a chain. In the wild, Asian elephants use their massive bodies to topple trees and their nimble trunks to move logs. Like trees, tractor tires are big and heavy. Heavy things allow elephants to work their powerful muscles by pushing and pulling.

PUSH

FLIP

Bozie plays with a small block feeder. Hay cubes are hidden inside. While working to get them out, she exercises the many different muscles in her trunk. She turns, flips, and shakes the feeder until every last bit of food falls out.

SCRATCH!

Elephants are very strong. Their enrichment feeders and toys must be "elephant-proof." Securing the items in such a way that the elephants can interact with but not break them is a challenge. It may take several keepers just to hang up one toy!

Tree trunks to scratch against, pools to bathe in, and new puzzles to solve keep elephant minds and bodies healthy. Sharing these experiences strengthens the elephants' bonds with one another too.

Another way keepers engage elephants is through training.
This keeps the elephants active and busy and teaches them to
trust their keepers. When the elephants carry out new behaviors
correctly, their keepers reward them with favorite foods.
This lets them know they've done a good job.

Visitors watch
the elephants
demonstrate their
behaviors. At right,
Rani presents her
side so keepers can
examine her up
close. She knows
her reward will be
a delicious apple.

Keepers also train the elephants to cooperate while having their blood drawn. Blood samples give veterinarians important information about each elephant's health. They also check the blood of the females, called cows, to know when it's time for them to breed. If all goes according to plan, Rani and Spike will someday mate, and their baby elephant, called a calf, will join the herd.

FWAAAAMP!

An elephant's trunk helps it "know" its world. A trunk performs many jobs, such as feeding, smelling, touching, making sounds, snorkeling, sifting, sorting, lifting, and pushing. Elephants also use their trunks for protection.

Kamala and Rani spend time together in their habitat.

Kamala trumpets to the herd. Zoo visitors love to hear the elephants call!

Asian elephants also snort, squeal, click, and purr. They can even make noises that humans can't hear. Low rumbles come from deep inside their throats. These send vibrations that other elephants can feel many miles away. This is how elephants send messages to each other.

Touch and body language are other important ways of communicating. Linking trunks can be a sign of friendship. Lifted tusks show power. Head bobs, ear flaps, and raised tails are all ways elephants talk to each other.

Kamala, Rani, Bozie, Swarna, and Spike follow the afternoon sun. Training is done for the day. The elephants might nap in a warm sunny spot, take a dip in the pool, or hang out with one another. They may go check out one of the timed feeders that keepers set. These provide food at random times throughout the day and night. Elephants learn quickly, so the keepers make sure to offer plenty of new games and challenges to the intelligent animals in their care.

Asian elephants spend about three-quarters of each day eating or moving toward a food or water source.

After a long day, the sun sets over the Zoo. The nighttime Zoo animals begin to stir, and the elephants settle in for the night.

The elephants might lie down to sleep, or they can sleep while standing. They have strong leg bones to support their great weight. Their legs are stacked under their bodies in a way that allows them to stand for long periods without using much energy.

ZZZZZZ....

There are no predators to disturb the Zoo elephants. Bozie, Swarna, Kamala, Rani, and Spike will get all the rest they need. In the morning, they'll wake up ready for another day. What surprises will the keepers have in store for them? Every day brings new adventures for this elephant family!

FACTS ABOUT ASIAN ELEPHANTS

Asian elephants (*Elephas maximus*) live in forests and grasslands in 13 countries in South and Southeast Asia. They typically weigh between 6,000 and 12,000 pounds (2,720 and 5,440 kg) and typically stand 6 to 12 feet (1.8 to 3.7 m) tall at the shoulder. In the wild, Asian elephants live in small herds of related females, their female offspring, and young males. They are extremely social and work together to raise their young and to protect the group. Unlike African elephants, they do not have a matriarch, or female leader. However, individual females will sometimes take on a more dominant role.

Wild Asian elephants graze grasses and browse leaves and woody plants for up to 18 hours a day. The area used by an elephant over the course of days and months is called a home range. It can vary in size from 6 to 20 square miles (15 to 50 square kilometers) to 190 to 580 square miles (500 to 1,500 sq km). In a typical day, they walk less than 4 miles (6.4 km). They need great amounts of food—165 to 330 pounds (75 to 150 kg) per day—and about 50 gallons (189 liters) of water. A very large male might eat twice that amount. This makes 200 pounds (90 kg) of poop and 13 gallons (49 L) of pee per elephant each day!

An elephant's trunk might be its most amazing feature. The trunk has about 150,000 muscle units and tendons, which provide the elephant precision as well as strength of movement. Trunks can suck up almost 2 gallons (7.6 L) of water per second that elephants either drink or spout over their heads for a shower. But trunks are also good at more delicate tasks. They can sniff out tasty foods to eat. They can suction up thin leaves. They can pluck up tiny nuts, their tips working like fingers. And maybe best of all, trunks can be used to greet, caress, and comfort other elephants.

Wild Asian elephants have been poached for their tusks, known as ivory. Among Asian elephants, only some males have large tusks. Other males and all females have small tusks that are usually hidden. These are called tushes. Trading in ivory between countries has been banned since 1990. But some people still want it for making trinkets and adding to traditional medicines. Because of ivory poaching, elephants with tusks have become more rare. Males use their tusks to fight each other and to show females they make good mates. How will their behaviors change without tusks? Scientists aren't sure yet. People need to better protect all elephants, including those with tusks, to ensure the species survives.

Asian elephants are endangered in the wild. Fewer than 50,000 remain in the world. There are about 2,000 in Myanmar, 1,500 in Borneo, fewer than 4,000 in Sri Lanka, and other small populations in India, China, Vietnam, Nepal, and other countries. The loss of forests, poaching for skin and meat, and other conflicts with humans are the biggest threats to these elephants. If left to roam and thrive, Asian elephants may live into their mid-50s.

GLOSSARY

anxious—afraid or nervous

bamboo—a type of tall grass with a woody stem; about 85 percent of an Asian elephant's diet is bamboo

browse—to eat leaves; Asian elephants browse for food about 18 hours a day

bull—adult male elephant; a male elephant typically leaves his mother's herd when he is about 12 years old; a bull, or bachelor, may grow up to live with other bulls or on his own

calf—baby elephant

cow—adult female elephant

endangered—a species at risk of disappearing from the wild

enrichment—activities that allow animals to demonstrate their species-typical behavior, give them opportunity to exercise control or choice over their environment, and improve their well-being

forage—to look for food

habitat—the area where an animal lives

mate—to join with another to produce young

Myanmar—a country in Southeast Asia also known as Burma; Myanmar borders India, Bangladesh, Laos, China, and Thailand

nimble—able to move with quick or delicate motions

orangutan—an ape with reddish-brown hair, about the size of a gorilla

pedicure—a treatment for the feet, toes, and toenails

poach—to illegally kill an animal for its meat, skin, tusks, or other body parts

Sri Lanka—a country in the Indian Ocean off the southeastern coast of India

Thailand—a country in southeastern Asia

vibration—a trembling motion that moves through air or ground

ABOUT THE AUTHOR

LELA NARGI is a journalist who also writes books and articles about science for kids. Her first picture book, *The Honeybee Man*, was a Junior Library Guild Selection, an NSTA "Outstanding Book," and a Bank Street Cook Prize honoree. She's also the author of National Geographic's *Absolute Expert: Dinosaurs* and *Absolute Expert: Volcanoes*, as well as Capstone's Mysteries of Space series and *Karl's New Beak*, a California Reading Association Eureka honoree and a best STEM book of 2020 by the National Science Teaching Association and The Children's Book Council. She lives in Brooklyn, New York.

Published by Capstone Editions, an imprint of Capstone
1710 Roe Crest Drive, North Mankato, Minnesota 56003
capstonepub.com

Library of Congress Cataloging-in-Publication Data is available on the Library of Congress website.
ISBN: 9781684465385 (hardcover)
ISBN: 9781684465408 (ebook PDF)

Summary: Rumble and mumble. Trumpet and stomp! Meet Kamala, Rani, Bozie, Swarna, and Spike! These busy Asian elephants have formed a family at Smithsonian's National Zoo and Conservation Biology Institute. Discover a day in the life of this elephant herd, how keepers interact with them, and how this work helps wild elephants thousands of miles away. Created in collaboration with the Smithsonian Institution, this fact-filled picture book will help young learners get to know these incredible creatures.

Editorial Credits
Editor: Kristen Mohn; Designer: Sarah Bennett; Media Researcher: Svetlana Zhurkin;
Production Specialist: Katy Lavigne

Our very special thanks to Tony Barthel, Curator of Elephant Trails, Smithsonian's National Zoo; Deborah Flinkman, Elephant Keeper, Smithsonian's National Zoo; Peter Leimgruber, Head of Conservation Ecology Center, Smithsonian Conservation Biology Institute; Jen Zoon, Communications Specialist. Capstone would also like to thank Kealy Gordon, Product Development Manager, and the following at Smithsonian Enterprises: Jill Corcoran, Director, Licensed Publishing; Brigid Ferraro, Vice President, Education and Consumer Products; and Carol LeBlanc, President, Smithsonian Enterprises.

Image Credits
Shutterstock: Bene_A, 29, EQRoy, 19, Francisca Alma Alvial (leaf background), cover and throughout, Helen E. Grose, 28 (top), LeksusTuss (grunge background), cover and throughout, LudmilaM, endsheets, Nilanka Sampath, 6, Paulaparaula (elephant footprints), 4–5, Santhosh Varghese, 30, tdee photo cm, 28 (bottom), Vintage Tone, 2–3 (sky); Smithsonian Institution: Abby Wood, 7, Adam Mason, cover (left and bottom right), 2 (left), 4 (top and middle), 18, 20, 23, 25 (top right), 26 (bottom left), Amy Enchelmeyer, 16, Connor Mallon, 3 (bottom), 4 (bottom), 17, 26–27 (back), Deborah Flinkman, 10 (bottom), Kayleigh Sullivan, 8, 14, Marie Galloway, 12, Paige Babel, 14–15, Rebecca Riley, 10 (top), Roshan Patel, cover (top right), back cover, 2–3, 5 (top), 11, 13, 27 (bottom right), Skip Brown, cover (middle right), 5 (bottom), 9, 21, 22, 24–25

Printed and bound in China. 4966